The Worst Team in the WORLD

Alan MacDonald

Illustrated by John Eastwood

OXFORD

1

Don't panic!

Reject Rovers were losing. Nothing new in that, but now they were on the attack. It always made their forwards nervous, especially Kevin 'Panic' Taylor.

By pure luck the ball had landed at his feet and he was wondering what to do with it. Kevin was just outside the penalty area and had a clear run on goal.

Coxley Colts' goalkeeper got hopefully to his feet. He'd been sitting down, bored to death for the last fifty minutes, without a single shot to save.

He came off his line and crouched ready to fling himself at Kevin's shot – if it ever came.

'Steady. No need to panic. Keep calm,' Kevin told himself.

He could see the back of the net and imagined the way it would quiver when the ball went in. If only he could just keep cool and for once – just for once – score a goal for Rovers.

'Shoot, Kevin! Shoot!' shouted Mr Turnbull from the touchline.

'Pass, Kevin!' yelled Persil.

Kevin looked up. He would have liked to pass. Someone else could gladly have the job of shooting. But as usual Persil was hovering way out by the corner flag.

He never came near the penalty area in case he got his kit dirty. It was all down to Kevin.

He could hear Colts' defenders pounding back to tackle him. Any second now a leg would lunge out and scoop the ball away to safety. The chance would be gone. It was now or never.

Kevin glanced up at the goal to take aim. And that was when the familiar panic set in. The goal seemed to shrink to Subbuteo size and the crouching goalkeeper grew hands like shovels.

Kevin felt hot and dizzy. He was sweating. When he swung his right leg back it felt like it was set in concrete. His toe connected with something hard ... it was the ground and Kevin fell flat on his face. The ball trundled harmlessly into the goalkeeper's gloves. (Kevin saw the disappointment on his face.)

'That's why they call you Thunderbolt, Captain!' called Persil from the wing.

Kevin didn't bother to answer. At least he'd got his kit dirty. In fact, his shirt and shorts were plastered in mud.

The Colts' goalkeeper kicked the ball upfield. It bounced once on the halfway line. Stringbean, Rejects' central defender, jumped to head it, but too early. His lanky body – all knees and elbows – went down as the ball was going up. It bounced over his head and one of Colts' strikers ran on to collect it.

There was only Rejects' goalkeeper, Scuba, to beat. He stayed on his line.

Scuba never came out in case someone dribbled round him and made him look stupid. He preferred to look stupid in his goal. But he always dived with great style – that's why the team called him Scuba.

The Colts' striker shot and the ball soared towards the right hand top corner.

Scuba dived spectacularly towards the bottom left hand corner. The ball bulged in the net.

The Colts' striker grinned and shook his head in disbelief. He shook hands with his team mates. There wasn't too much celebration. After all, it was his fifth goal that afternoon and the score was 11-0. The referee blew his whistle soon after.

'Bad luck, lad,' he said to Kevin, picking up the match ball. 'Someone's got to lose. You lot make it look easy.'

'Yeah,' said Kevin, 'we've had a lot of practice.'

They trudged off the pitch miserably.

'Why didn't you score? You had an open goal!' Scuba moaned to Kevin.

'The ball bobbled. The pitch was hopeless,' scowled Kevin.

'Not as hopeless as you. What use is a captain who panics every time he sees the goal?'

'What use is a goalkeeper who always dives the wrong way?' Kevin snapped back. 'We'd do better with a stuffed dummy in goal. At least it would keep still.'

'No point you two arguing,' said Mr
Turnbull, Scuba's dad. 'You were just unlucky,
that's all. The slope was against you in the
second half.'

Kevin caught Scuba's eye and almost
grinned. They knew Mr Turnbull had been
reading his newspaper for most of the match.

He always said the same thing. Whether
the score was 5-0 or 22-0, Rovers were always
unlucky according to Mr Turnbull.

He only came because Rovers used his builder's van as their team coach.

It was a good job their kit was red; it didn't show the brick dust too badly.

'You never lost *again*, did you?' a mocking voice called behind them.

Kevin turned his head to see Sean Slack. Slack played for Eastley Dynamos who had been playing on the next pitch.

Dynamos were top of the District Junior League, as Slack never missed a chance to remind them. He was the last person Kevin wanted to talk to right now.

'Don't you want to be with your own team?' Kevin asked.

'S'all right,' said Slack. 'I just wanted to know how you got on. Out of interest.'

'I suppose you won again?' asked Scuba, avoiding the question.

'Four-one,' said Slack. 'I scored a hat-trick, if you're interested. It could have been more but I'm saving myself for our next game.'

'Why? Who are you playing?'

Even as he asked the question Kevin knew the answer.

'Don't you know? We're playing you in two weeks' time. It's going to be a massacre. I've told the ref to bring his pocket calculator to keep the score.'

Kevin let out a silent groan. Scuba closed his eyes. He was imagining picking the ball out of the net every ten seconds for an entire match.

'Anyway,' said Slack, as neither of them spoke, 'you haven't answered my question.'

'What question?' said Kevin. He was trying to run on ahead.

Slack kept up with him. 'Today. Did you lose? Again?'

'Yes.'

'What was the score then?'

'Eleven-nil,' said Kevin. 'It could have been more but we're saving ourselves for our next game.'

They'd reached the pavilion. With relief, Kevin and Scuba went inside.

But Slack followed them into the changing room. He hadn't finished rubbing it in.

'So tell me again. How many games is that you've lost in a row?'

'Get lost, Slack! We're getting changed!' said Kevin.

'But how many? Just tell me, then I'll go. Have you won any games this season?'

'No!'

'Drawn any?'

'No!'

'So you've lost *every single* game?'

'I just said so. Now get out!'

'And you lost them all last season. So how many games is that all together?'

'Why does it matter? What's it to you?'

'I just want to know.'

'Thirty-nine games, okay?'

Sean Slack whistled.

'Thirty-nine defeats in a row. Is that some sort of record? You could be the worst team in the world.'

'Get lost, Slackpants!'

Slack retreated out of the doorway in a hail of football boots and shin pads.

He made his way back to Dynamos' changing room, grinning to himself and shaking his head. 'Thirty-nine games in a row. Maybe that *is* a record. I'll have to look it up.'

2

On the record

Sean Slack found his dad's *Guinness Book of Records* on the bottom shelf of the bookcase. He wiped the dusty cover with his sleeve. It was ages since he'd looked at the book.

He looked at the world's longest beard (over five metres), the world's biggest hamburger (two and a half tonnes) and the world's busiest dentist (pulled out two million teeth).

At last he found the football section near the back. There was the list of great winning teams. Man United, Liverpool, Tottenham, Arsenal ... But Sean wasn't interested in winners.

He was looking for the most hopeless team in football history. And there, at the bottom of page 124, he found them.

'The worst run of defeats was recorded by Doddering Old Boys. In the 1951-2 and 1952-3 seasons they lost thirty-nine games in a row. Their dreadful run finally came to an end with a 0-0 draw against Hardly Athletic.'

Thirty-nine games. Sean stroked his pointed nose thoughtfully.

So Reject Rovers weren't the worst team in history – yet. Unfortunately, somebody had got there first.

But Rovers had *already* lost thirty-nine games in a row. So they were only one game away from breaking the record. And that one game was against Sean's own team, Eastley Dynamos.

A thin smile spread across Sean's weasel face. Just two more weeks and he would help Reject Rovers to enter history as *the worst team of all time*. They'd never live it down. He could just see Kevin Taylor's face when he heard. And Sean would make sure the news got around.

He hadn't forgotten what had happened three years ago. Kevin Taylor had just started Rovers when Sean had generously offered to be their captain. It had been put to the vote and they'd actually turned him down. Him! – Sean Slack – with more talent in his big toe than their whole team put together.

The insult of being rejected by a bunch of rejects still made him smart with anger. Ever since he'd been waiting to get even. Now the perfect chance had fallen into his lap.

As he put the book back on the shelf Sean's eyes fell on the local paper. It lay open at the sports page.

There was the usual round-up of the local leagues by someone called Steve Ryan.

It gave Sean an idea, an idea so brilliant he had to go out to the hall mirror and blow a big kiss to himself. Reject Rovers were about to become famous!

Kevin Taylor had no idea that fame was about to call on him. At that moment he was more worried about his poster collection.

'You can put them up in the spare bedroom,' his mum told him for the third time.

'I don't want to put them up there,' Kevin protested. 'I want them here. In *my* bedroom. They're all in the right order.'

'Kevin. What's the difference? You're just being awkward about this.'

Kevin flopped down on his bed. He knew he was being awkward but he had a right to be. This was his bedroom. It had always been his bedroom. And now his mum wanted to give it to some lodger and move him into the spare room.

'Why can't *he* go in the spare room? I live here. I was here first.'

'I've told you, the spare room's too small,' said Kevin's mum. 'And I want him to have a bit of privacy. In the top room he can get away from you and your sister arguing all the time.'

'We don't argue all the time!' argued Kevin. 'We only argue when she's wrong.'

His sister Fiona was thirteen, an age when there ought to be a ban on sisters, in Kevin's opinion.

With alarm, Kevin saw his mum starting to peel one of his posters off the wall.

'Don't do that!' yelled Kevin. 'You'll get them mixed up.' His football posters were arranged in a special order.

They started with his favourite team, Man Utd, over his bed. The teams then ran along the wall to his tenth favourite, Raith Rovers (same initials as Rejects) over the radiator.

Gloomily, Kevin started to take them down while his mum cleared out the wardrobe.

'Anyway, I still don't see why we need a lodger.'

'I've told you. We need the extra money now I'm only working part-time.'

'What if I don't like him?' said Kevin.

'He sounds a perfectly nice young man. His name's Alex. He's a student teacher at Grimley High.'

'A teacher?' groaned Kevin. 'You didn't say he was a teacher!'

'Didn't I? What's wrong with that?'

'He'll talk about tadpoles and magnets. He'll want us to line up for breakfast!'

'Don't be silly, Kevin. I bet you'll like him.'

'Oh yeah? What team does he support?'

'How do I know? He may not even like football. There are people in this universe, believe it or not, Kevin, who manage to live without football.'

'Only boring ones,' Kevin muttered. 'Didn't you ask him any questions? He could be an axe murderer. He could be planning to chop us all in pieces while we sleep.'

'As long as he washes the sheets afterwards,' said Kevin's mum, absently.

Kevin took down his last team poster (Bournemouth – he'd been there on holiday) and looked around. His room already looked bare and empty – not like his room at all.

He felt sure he was going to hate Alex. He had enough of teachers at school.

His thoughts were suddenly interrupted by the phone ringing. Thumping downstairs, Kevin picked up the receiver. A voice said: 'Hello, does Mr Taylor live there?'

'You want my mum. She's upstairs,' said Kevin.

'No I don't. It's a Mr Kevin Taylor I want to speak to.'

Kevin hesitated. He tried to think what he'd done wrong recently. What trouble could he be in? It didn't sound like his headteacher, Mr Rees, whose voice could shatter windows. This voice was smooth and friendly.

'That's me. I'm Kevin Taylor,' he answered at last.

'Oh! It's just you sounded rather young. I was told you manage a football team called Rocket Rovers.'

'Reject Rovers,' corrected Kevin. 'I'm player manager. And captain too.'

'Right. Well my name's Steve Ryan. I'm a sports reporter with *The Grimley Gazette*. I was wondering if we could come and do a report on your team.'

Kevin was stunned. Speechless.

'Hello? Are you still there?' asked Ryan.

'Yes … yes … yes, of course,' Kevin stammered.

'You mean "yes" we can do the report?'

'Yes,' said Kevin. He was sounding like a recorded message.

'Great! I'd like to get the whole team together. Take some pics. Are you training or anything this evening?'

'Oh yes,' Kevin lied, 'we train every evening over at Riverside Park.'

'Great. I'll meet you there in about an hour.'

Kevin put the phone down in shock. How had *The Grimley Gazette* got to know about Reject Rovers? And why on earth were they interested in a team as hopeless as them? Kevin couldn't imagine.

Picking up the phone again he dialled Scuba's number. Wait till the rest of the team heard about this. They were going to get their pictures in the paper – just like Man Utd!

3

Facing the press

All the Rovers team were at the park by the time Kevin got there. In fact, most of them had been waiting half an hour.

'Where's the reporter?' asked Scuba anxiously.

'He said he'd meet us here. What are those for?' Kevin pointed to Scuba's dark glasses.

'I thought they'd look cool. You know, for the pictures.'

'You're supposed to be our goalkeeper – not a film star,' grumbled Kevin. He sniffed the air. 'And what's that awful smell? Like cat's pee.'

'It's Persil. He's wearing his dad's aftershave.'

Kevin was about to make a speech about acting like a serious football team when a red car drew up. Out got Steve Ryan and the photographer from *The Grimley Gazette*.

Ryan turned out to be a spotty young man in a brown suit much too large for him. He strode towards them briskly with his hand outstretched.

'Steve Ryan. *Grimley Gazette*. Which one of you is Kevin?'

'I am,' said Kevin, stepping forward to shake his hand. He felt important talking to a real reporter.

'Great, Kev. This is Ted. He's going to be taking the pics.'

Ted winked and showed them a large camera.

'Okay, lads?' he said. They all nodded eagerly.

'Do you want to take the photos now?' asked Scuba, adjusting his dark glasses. 'I could go in goal and dive around a bit.'

Ryan shook his head. 'We'll do that later. First I'd like to ask Kev a few questions about the team. Shall we sit down somewhere?'

Kevin followed Ryan over to a park bench. The rest of the Rovers team went too. They had never seen a reporter and they were anxious not to miss anything.

It ended up with twelve of them squashed onto one bench.

It took several minutes for Kevin to get them all off. At last they were ready to start the interview.

'Now,' said Steve Ryan, getting out his notebook. 'Reject Rovers. That's a pretty unusual name for a football team. Why did you choose it?'

'It was kind of a joke to start with,' began Kevin. 'None of us had a team to play for so me, Scuba and Stringbean, we thought...'

'Scuba and Stringbean?' Ryan's pencil had stopped scribbling.

'Yeah, they're nicknames. We've all got them. It's sort of a club rule.' He pointed out the members of the team. 'Persil, VJ, Dangerous, Baby Joe ...'

'Baby Joe?'

'Because he can't stop dribbling ... Do you want to write them all down?' asked Kevin.

'Er, maybe later. You were saying how you got the name Rejects ...'

'Oh yes. Me, Scuba and Stringbean decided to start our own team. And we called ourselves Reject Rovers because ... well, no other teams wanted us.'

''Cos we're all useless,' put in Stringbean, helpfully. Kevin glared at him to shut up.

'And how long exactly have Rovers been together?' asked Ryan.

'This is our third season. We're still improving. The best is yet to come,' said Kevin. He'd heard a manager say that once on TV and thought it sounded good.

'But what about results, Kev? Rovers haven't won too many games this season, have they?'

'We've had a lot of bad luck,' admitted Kevin.

'Dodgy referees,' said Scuba.

'And Kevin keeps missing the goal!' added Stringbean.

Kevin shot him another withering look. He was hoping Steve Ryan didn't want to ask too many questions about Rovers' dismal record. But that was exactly the kind of detail he seemed interested in.

Kevin knew the figures for this season off by heart. *Played 19, Won 0, Drawn 0, Lost 19, Goals for: 3, Goals against: 104.*

'So if you lost all twenty games last season and nineteen this season, that means you've lost thirty-nine games in a row, Kev. That's right isn't it, thirty-nine?'

Kevin had to admit it was, though he wished Ryan would stop repeating it.

'You don't have to put that in the report, do you?' he asked. 'We don't want people to think … you know, we're useless.'

'No, no, of course not!' Ryan fingered a spot on his chin. 'This is just background stuff, Kev. Reporters have to check out all these little facts, you know.'

After that Ted wanted to take some pictures. He suggested they just do their normal training session while he snapped a few shots.

Rovers looked blankly at their manager. *Training sessions?* They never had training sessions, only the occasional kickabout.

Kevin thought quickly. 'Line up,' he said. 'We'll start with penalty practice.'

There was a lot of pushing and shoving to be at the front of the queue. Everyone wanted their picture in the paper.

Stringbean got there first. He played for a junior basketball team and was a head taller than the rest.

He took a long run-up, almost to the halfway line, and charged at the ball like an express train.

His shot sailed into orbit about thirty metres over the crossbar. Even Scuba didn't bother to dive.

Ted's camera went click. 'Nice try,' he said and gave them another wink.

Persil was next. No one had ever actually asked him to shoot before. He took a few steps forward and scuffed the ball gently along the ground. It didn't even reach the goal.

Then it was Kevin's turn. He was beginning to wonder if taking pictures was such a good idea after all. But it was up to him, as player manager, to show that Rovers were not a joke team.

He placed the ball carefully on the spot. Ted moved in a step closer to get a good shot of him. Scuba crouched low, ready to dive. Kevin began his run up. At the last minute he looked up at the goal. That was his big mistake. Panic took over. What if he missed? What if he made an idiot of himself?

Gripped by fear, he completely forgot to look down at the ball. His foot swung wildly and he spun round like a top. When he looked again the ball was exactly where it had been before.

'Did you get that one, Ted?' grinned Steve Ryan.

Ted winked back. 'Great stuff,' he said. 'Now just a few of the goalkeeper. Why don't you give him a few shots, Steve?'

Steve Ryan lined up his first shot. Scuba could hardly see the ball through his dark glasses.

The first shot hit him on the nose and sent the glasses spinning into the air.

The second shot hit the post and cannoned off the back of his head into the net.

Scuba let in seven out of seven. Ted took lots of pictures.

Last of all, they lined up for a team photo. Ted organized them in two rows, arms folded, just like Man Utd.

'Well thanks a lot, lads,' said Steve Ryan. 'I think we've got what we wanted.'

'Will we be in the paper tomorrow?' asked Kevin.

'We'll try and make the late edition. Anyway, good luck with the next game, lads. You'll need it I reckon.'

'Yeah, we haven't a hope,' said Kevin. 'Not against Eastley Dynamos. They're top of the league.'

'And that Sean's a useful striker I'm told.'

'Sean Slack?'

'That's the one. Twenty-one goals this season.'

'Who told you that?'

'Oh, one of you must have mentioned it. Ready for the off then, Ted?'

Ryan and Ted thanked them and said goodbye.

Kevin thought about it afterwards. He couldn't remember anyone talking about Sean Slack.

4

The fame game

Kevin had told everyone at school that
Rovers were going to be in *The Grimley
Gazette*. He hadn't meant to, he just couldn't
help it. Miles Elliot had been showing off in
the playground.

Miles was one of Sean Slack's gang. He
played for Eastley Dynamos and Kevin
couldn't stand him. Miles boasted that his
uncle had been on the radio talking about
bird-watching or something.

Kevin had waited until Miles had finished
boasting. Then he'd dropped his bombshell.

'Matter of fact, I was just talking to Steve
Ryan last night.'

'Who is Steve Ryan?' asked Miles, rolling his eyes.

'Don't you know who Steve Ryan is, Miles? I thought you knew something about football. Steve Ryan writes the sports page for *The Grimley Gazette*. He phoned me up last night.'

Kevin could tell no one believed him. But luckily Scuba was there to back him up. Soon they were telling the whole story. By lunchtime it was all round the school.

Kevin Taylor had been interviewed for the paper. Reject Rovers were going to be in *The Grimley Gazette*. There would be pictures. Kevin had been driven home in a silver Rolls Royce. (He'd got a bit carried away with the story.)

As the day went on, Kevin's fame grew and grew. He noticed younger kids at school whispering and pointing. When he was lining up for dinner, a first year tugged at his sleeve. The small boy pushed a pencil and a piece of paper at Kevin.

'What's this for?'

'Autograph,' said the boy.

'What?'

'You're the boy that's gonna be in the papers?'

'Yeah, that's me.'

'Well, can I have your autograph? I collect them.'

Kevin had signed his name, laughing, but it felt good. At last he was somebody at school. Everyone knew his name. He began to imagine what his photo would look like in the paper.

'Kevin Taylor, manager.' Or 'Kevin Taylor, player manager of Rovers.' Better still, 'Kevin Taylor, Rovers' ace striker.'

* * *

It was Sean Slack who first got hold of *The Grimley Gazette*. He'd run all the way to the paper shop straight after school. Kevin was coming out of the school gates. A crowd of admirers were with him.

'Have you seen it?' said Slack, running up out of breath.

'Seen what?'

'The paper.' He waved it under Kevin's face.

'Is it in there?' asked Kevin eagerly.

'Oh yes, it's in there all right. A big report. All over the back page.'

Kevin grabbed the paper. He wondered why Slack was looking so pleased. Turning to the back page, he found out. The headline was in big bold letters over a team photo of Rovers: **'Is This The Worst Team in History?'** The article by Steve Ryan said:

'Next week, a local boys' team, Reject Rovers, will make football history. If they lose the match they'll have lost forty games in a row. Forty! That's a record. According to the Guinness Book of Records *it will earn them the title of "The Worst Team of All Time". No wonder they call themselves the Rejects! I went to see them in training and I soon found out what makes Rovers so hopeless ...'*

Kevin's eyes skipped to the photos below –
the ball pinging off Scuba's nose,

Stringbean watching his shot enter a distant
galaxy, and him – Kevin 'Panic' Taylor
kicking thin air. *'Whoops! Missed again, Kevin!'*
said the caption.

Kevin lowered the paper in horror, unable
to read on. Why hadn't anyone told him?

They'd been tricked. The report made them sound like a joke. They were about to become famous as *The Worst Team in History*. No wonder Steve Ryan had wanted to meet them!

Kevin's mind raced ahead. What would the rest of the team say when they saw this? They were bound to blame him – their manager. After all, he'd brought Ryan to see them. And what about the others? His friends, his class, everyone at school?

By tomorrow morning nearly everyone would have seen the paper. They were bound to. He'd told them all to buy a copy.

Miles Elliot grabbed the paper from his hand. The others crowded round to see.

'There's Kevin!'

'Look at his face! What a moron!'

'He can't even kick the ball!'

'Good, isn't it?' said Sean Slack. 'I mean, I think people should know just how useless you lot are. The most useless team in history. You could put that on your shirts.'

Kevin saw the look of cruel triumph on
Slack's face. Suddenly he understood.

'It was you, wasn't it?' he said. He pushed
his face into Slack's. 'You set this all up. You
phoned the paper. You told Steve Ryan all
about us.'

Slack tried to push him away. He backed
off a few steps.

'Don't be dumb! Think I'd go to all that
trouble? Just for your pathetic team?'

'So how come he knew about you?'

'Who did?'

'Steve Ryan. He knew your name.'

'So what?'

'He even knew how many goals you'd scored this season. Twenty-one.'

Slack's eyes betrayed his mistake.

'You're mad. He could have easily found that out himself.'

'Why should he? You couldn't help showing off, could you, Slackpants?'

Sean Slack looked round for support. The crowd around them had closed in. They sensed a fight. But Slack didn't want that. He wanted Kevin to look stupid.

'At least I've got something to show off about,' he taunted. 'Not like the worst team in history.'

'We're not. Not yet.'

'But you will be. When we thrash you.'

'*If* you thrash us,' said Kevin rashly.

'Oh yeah! You reckon we won't? You lot are so slow a team of snails could beat you!'

That was when Kevin made his big mistake. He should have turned around and walked away then.

He should have said something clever like, 'I'd rather play snails than a slug like you.' But that's not what he said.

With everyone watching, he went up to Sean Slack and held out his hand.

'Want a bet?' he demanded.

'What? Who'll win on Saturday?' said Slack.

'Yeah. If you're so sure.'

'You're on.' Slack took his hand. 'And the loser has to clean the other player's boots ...'

'All right,' agreed Kevin.

'... by licking the mud off,' added Slack.

'You must be joking! I'm not licking your boots.'

'Too late,' said Slack. 'We just shook on the bet.' He turned to the others. 'You all saw that didn't you?'

The others nodded in agreement. Kevin was shaking hands when Slack had spoken. There was no way out. The bet was made.

The crowd round him was grinning. They couldn't wait to see him eat dirt.

'Anyway, you haven't won yet. We'll see on the day,' said Kevin weakly. He walked away on his own. The others stayed behind with Sean Slack.

As he crossed to the other side of the road Slack's voice reached him. 'Hey, Taylor! I nearly forgot – give us your autograph will ya?'

5

Lose the lodger

Kevin booted a stone into the gutter. What had he done? He'd just bet that Rovers would win on Saturday. He might as well have bet that he'd be the first man on Mars. It was impossible. Hopeless.

They'd be lucky if they kept the score down to less than ten. And then what? As far as Kevin could see his whole life would be ruined. Rovers would be for ever known as the worst team in history. The team that had lost a record forty games in a row.

They'd have to split up. Who would want to play for them? They'd be a joke.

You'd only have to mention the name, Reject Rovers, and everyone would fall about laughing.

All that was bad enough. It had taken a genius to make it worse. The bet with Slack was the most stupid thing that Kevin had ever done.

He could picture the moment after the match. Eastley Dynamos would be slapping each other on the back. Rovers would be trailing off the pitch, heads down. Then Slack would step forward with a big smirk on his face. There, in front of everyone, he would remind Kevin of their bet.

He'd take off his muddy boots, hand them over and say, 'Lick them clean, Taylor. Go on!'

Kevin wondered if he could move to the North Pole before next week. Maybe it was too cold for football there.

He opened the back door and drooped into the kitchen. Someone was sitting at the table having coffee with his mum. Kevin didn't even glance at them.

'Ah, here's Kevin. How was school?' asked his mum.

'Don't ask,' said Kevin.

'Bad as that? Never mind, I've got someone I'd like you to meet. This is our new lodger, Alex.'

Kevin had completely forgotten that the lodger was arriving today. That was all he needed.

He turned to look properly at the person sitting with his mum.

It was a girl. Older than Kevin's sister but not *old* like his mum.

She had dark frizzy hair. It was tied back in a red band but lots of it seemed to be escaping. The girl held out her hand to Kevin, beaming at him.

'Hi, Kevin. I'm Alex.'

Kevin opened and shut his mouth like a goldfish. 'But you're ... you're ... not a man.'

'I know. Sorry about that. It's my name you see. Alex. I should have said in my letter that Alex is short for Alexandria. People often expect me to be a man.'

Kevin's mum nodded. 'I'd even had a shaving point fitted in the bathroom.' They both went into fits of giggles.

'Great,' said Kevin. 'Just great. Well that makes it a perfect day.'

He dumped his bag on the floor and stomped upstairs to his bedroom. Kevin's mum sighed. 'Sorry about that. He can be so rude sometimes. But he'll get used to you.'

* * *

Kevin lay on his bed, staring at the ceiling. It was just the final straw. He'd just had the worst day of his life at school, he'd made a stupid bet, and now the lodger turned out to be a girl. With his mum and his sister, that meant he'd be out-numbered three to one in the house.

His sister was bound to love Alex. She'd probably borrow her make-up and start to talk like her.

When Kevin wanted to watch the football on TV, Alex and his sister would want the other side – probably some mushy love story.

It wasn't fair. He didn't want a lodger in the first place. And he certainly didn't want one who was a teacher *and* a woman.

Why should he give up his bedroom to Alex?

That was it. Why should he? He'd get rid of her. He'd think of a plan to make sure she *didn't* stay in the house. The idea almost made him forget about the match.

By the time his mum called him for supper, Kevin had put stage one of his plan into operation. He'd phoned Scuba and asked him to come round later.

Kevin said little at dinner. When Alex tried to ask friendly questions, he gave her short answers. He went to Grimley Park Primary. It was an okay school. Yes, he liked football.

'Kevin is manager of his own football team, aren't you, Kevin?' his mum said, encouragingly.

'Yeah,' said Kevin. 'But you wouldn't be interested. We're useless. Really useless.'

'I don't know. Maybe I could come and watch you sometime,' suggested Alex.

Kevin gave her a dark look. He had enough trouble without her poking her nose in. She probably thought West Ham was a kind of meat.

When Scuba arrived, Kevin smuggled him quickly upstairs to his bedroom.

'Have you got them?'

'Yeah,' said Scuba. 'They're in here. But you still haven't said what it's all about.'

'Let's see them,' said Kevin.

Scuba put the shoe box down on the bed. The lid had a row of air holes in it. Inside were his two brown pet mice, Salt and Pepper. They climbed over each other and sniffed the air.

'It's a shame they're not a bit bigger,' said Kevin.

'Why?'

'Rats,' whispered Kevin. 'She'll hate them. We're going to put them in her bed and wait for the screams.'

'In your sister's bed?'

'No, dumbo! I told you on the phone. It's this student teacher, Alex. She's the new lodger. If she thinks we've got rats in the house, she'll leave. She'll be out of here like a shot.'

Scuba stroked Pepper's fur. He looked doubtful.

'It'll work, you'll see. I'll be able to have my old room back,' said Kevin.

'But they're not rats, they're mice,' objected Scuba. 'And what if this Alex frightens them?'

'She won't. She'll take one look and run out of the house. Grown-ups are like that about rats. They've only got to see one and they go round the bend.'

They climbed the stairs quietly to Alex's room. Scuba had Salt and Pepper hidden under his jumper, but no one saw them.

Alex was still downstairs helping Kevin's mum to wash up. Scuba hid the mice just under the duvet. They were bound to come out and explore sooner or later.

Ten minutes later they heard Alex coming upstairs. They watched her from Kevin's bedroom, hiding behind the door.

Alex went into her room and closed her door. Kevin gave a thumbs-up sign to Scuba. They waited for the screams.

Five minutes passed. Ten. Twenty. After half an hour, Scuba started to worry. Not a sound was coming from upstairs. What if the lodger had accidentally sat on Salt or Pepper? What if she'd attacked them with a shoe?

'Perhaps she hasn't seen them yet,' said Kevin. 'We'll have to go in.'

'How?' said Scuba. 'We can't walk in and say, "Excuse me, have you seen the mice we left in your bed?"'

'We'll say we saw a rat. Then we can find them while she's on a chair, hollering.'

They crept upstairs and listened at the door. There was still no sound. Kevin banged on the door and flung it open.

'RATS!' he shrieked. 'We saw a big ugly rat come in here!'

Kevin stopped. Both of them stared.

Alex was sitting on her bed with Pepper on her shoulder. Salt was playing happily in her lap.

'It's okay. They're only mice,' she laughed. 'Aren't they great? Do they belong to you?'

Scuba was so relieved that his pets were unharmed, he completely forgot that Alex was supposed to be the enemy. Soon he was sitting on the bed, telling her all about his pets.

Kevin meanwhile was staring in amazement at his old room. Alex had already made a lot of changes. A guitar was propped in the corner. The walls were covered in posters of faraway places. Kevin's eye took in the Brazilian footballer with the ball at his feet.

Alex's blue tracksuit hung over a chair. There was a badge on the top pocket.

'What's this?' Kevin asked.

Alex looked up from playing with Scuba's mice.

'Oh, I'm very proud of that. It's my FA coaching badge.'

'FA? You mean football coaching?'

'That's it. I did it as part of my teacher training. It was great.

'I've always wanted to coach a football team. Pity they won't let me near the school team where I'm teaching.'

Scuba and Kevin looked at each other.

'You could coach us,' said Scuba.

'No, she couldn't,' Kevin said, quickly. 'We've already got a manager. Me.'

'But you don't know how to coach. We don't even have proper training sessions.'

'I'm the manager,' said Kevin. 'And we don't need any help.'

'Oh no, course we don't!' said Scuba. 'That's why we're bottom of the league. That's why we're going to get thrashed on Saturday. That's why we'll be the worst team of all time.'

'I saw today's paper,' admitted Alex. 'Will you really be breaking this record?'

Kevin nodded. 'Looks like it.'

'Unless we get a lot better,' said Scuba. 'And Alex could help us.'

'It's too late,' said Kevin. 'We've got less than two weeks left.'

Alex shrugged. 'It's your team. If you like I could watch you practise after school tomorrow. But it's up to you. You're the manager.'

'Kevin?' said Scuba.

Kevin scowled. 'I'll think about it,' he said.

6

Countdown to disaster

The next day at school started badly for
Kevin. When he walked into the classroom
he had the feeling that everyone was waiting
for him. He sat down in his seat. Something
was taped to the table.

His picture. The one from *The Grimley
Gazette* that showed him missing the ball
completely. '*Whoops! Missed again, Kevin!*',
the caption reminded him.

Kevin flushed red. He could hear
sniggering all round the classroom.

He swung round furiously and saw Sean Slack and Miles Elliot, doubled up with laughter.

'You think this is funny?' Kevin said to Slack, ripping up the picture.

'Not as funny as your face right now,' hooted Slack.

'Give us your autograph, Kevin!' jeered Miles.

'Oooh, Kevin! You're so famous!' sang Amanda Ross, pretending to faint.

Kevin sat back down. He got out his book and buried his face in it. He didn't want anyone to see he'd gone red. It wasn't fair. He'd get Sean Slack for this. He'd show him somehow.

But that was only the beginning. Slack had been busy.

Everywhere he went Kevin found the *Gazette* pictures on display. There was one over his peg in the cloakroom. There was one on the mirror in the boys' toilets.

When their teacher, Mrs Lock, opened the register, there was another. It was the team photo of Reject Rovers with the headline, '*Is This The Worst Team in History?*'

Mrs Lock asked Kevin if he had put it there. She couldn't understand why the whole class burst out laughing.

Worst of all was lunchtime. In the dinner queue everyone was sniggering at Kevin. It wasn't until he sat down that he discovered the piece of paper stuck to his back. In black felt pen someone had scrawled:

Worst manager in the WORLD

As soon as he got home Kevin ran upstairs. He slammed his door shut and buried his face in his pillow. If this was what life was going to be like he didn't want to go to school. He'd have to stay in his room for ever. Later there was a knock on his bedroom door.

'Go away!'

'Kevin? It's me, Alex.'

'Go away!'

Alex poked her head round the door. 'It's about training tonight. Do you want me to come ... or not?'

Kevin came out from his pillow. He'd forgotten Alex's offer. He hadn't even talked to any of Rovers about going training.

'What's the use?' he said. 'We're useless. The most useless team in history. And I'm the most useless manager. You ask anyone at school. They're all coming to watch us lose the match. Slack's told everyone.'

Alex came in and sat down on the side of his bed. 'Who's this Slack then?'

So Kevin told her. He told her all about Sean Slack and *The Grimley Gazette*. About the pictures that had appeared all round school. And about the stupid bet he'd made.

Alex listened. She was a good listener. She didn't interrupt like most people. At the end she said, 'So, there's only one way out.'

'What?' said Kevin hopelessly. He didn't see any way out.

'You just have to win the match. Then you won't be the worst team of all time, you'll be heroes. And Sean Slack will lose the bet. He'll be the one to look stupid instead of you.'

Kevin hadn't really thought of it like that. Alex was right. But there was one big problem. 'You haven't seen us play,' said Kevin. 'We'll never beat Slack's lot in a million years. That reporter was right – we're hopeless.'

'Let me be the judge of that,' said Alex. 'Come on, get your kit on. And tell the others they're going training.'

An hour later Rovers' players were gathered
at Riverside Park. Alex came in her tracksuit.
She let Kevin introduce her to the rest of the
team.

They started with a game of five-a-side, so
that Alex could watch them play.

Kevin kicked off. He passed the ball to
Baby Joe. Baby Joe went on a long dribble
that took him past five players and back to
where he started. Persil hung out on the
wing, shouting, 'Pass! Pass!' When the ball
eventually came to him, he passed to
Stringbean. It would have been a good pass if
Stringbean had been on the same side.
Stringbean did what he always did, hoofed
the ball with all his might up the other end.

'Mine! Leave it!' shouted Scuba, coming out to catch the ball.

He collided with Dangerous who went for anything that moved. The ball bounced once and nestled in the net.

'Goal!' shouted Stringbean. 'At least we scored one.'

They all looked at Alex. Her mouth was still open. Kevin hadn't been exaggerating when he said that they were bad.

'Well, there's plenty to work on,' she said. Soon Alex had them dribbling in and out of rows of jumpers. They passed the ball in triangles with one touch. (Most of them had never received a pass from one of their own players.)

Scuba practised diving in goal. He discovered that when he kept his eyes open, he sometimes went the right way and saved a shot. They practised corners with Persil taking them. The tenth time Persil got the ball off the ground.

Kevin and Scuba jumped for it together.

The ball glanced off Kevin's head before he had time to panic. It hit the inside of the post and rebounded into the net.

'Goal!' said Kevin, astonished. 'I scored a goal ... didn't I?'

'A peach,' said Alex. 'A brilliant header from Persil's perfect cross.'

Persil glowed with pride. No one had ever praised him before.

'Now,' said Alex. 'Let's hear you say it: "We're Rovers. We're winners. We're the best."'

It took a few tries. Words like 'winners' and 'the best' were difficult to say. But after a lot of laughter, they managed it.

In the end they were chanting it all around the park. 'We're Rovers, we're winners, we're the best!'

'Good,' said Alex. 'We've made a start. But there's still a lot to work on. Back here for training tomorrow night.'

Someone else had been watching Rovers training.

As the voices faded away, two figures crawled out from the bushes.

'Ahh! I've got prickles in my leg,' said Miles Elliot.

'Never mind your leg, who was that in the tracksuit?' Sean Slack demanded.

'I don't know. Maybe it was Taylor's mum.'

'Don't be stupid!'

'Anyway, what are you worried about? We'll still murder them on Saturday. You saw. It took them ten corners before they got one in the goal.'

'Who said I was worried?' said Slack. 'We'd beat them if they had ten goals' start. Still ... we don't want to take any chances, do we?'

'How do you mean?'

'Well, I'm not having Taylor winning our bet. So I bought something just to make sure.'

Slack brought a tin out of his pocket and showed it to Miles.

Miles read the writing on the label and grinned horribly.

'Itching powder. Does it work?'

Slack nodded. 'Agony. The strongest stuff in the shop. It makes your eyes water and you can't stop scratching.'

'Who shall we try it on first?' asked Miles.

'I think it might help their goalkeeper, don't you?'

Slack bared his pointed teeth in a smile of pure pleasure.

7

A nasty itch

As the match drew near Kevin got more and more nervous. It seemed everyone in Grimley knew about Rovers and their record-breaking game.

Slack had made sure that the news was all around the school. The newspaper report had done the rest. Rovers' fame had spread far and wide. Kevin even had a phone call from a local TV producer who wanted to bring a camera crew to the match.

Alex had done her best. She had them out practising after school every day.

By the end of ten training sessions there were signs they were getting better. Scuba, in particular, had started to save shots instead of diving aimlessly. And for the first time they were passing the ball to each other.

Even Baby Joe had stopped trying to beat the whole team on his own.

Still, Kevin knew it wasn't enough. If they were playing someone else they might have had a slim chance, but not Eastley Dynamos. Eastley hadn't lost a game all season. Beating Rovers would make them league champions.

What's more, Kevin had seen Sean Slack play. Even he had to admit that Slack was the deadliest striker in the school.

No, Rovers would need a miracle to avoid defeat.

Kevin couldn't even bring himself to think about the bet and the humiliation that was in store for him. He could almost taste the dirt on Slack's boots. It was going to be the worst day of his whole life.

On Saturday morning Scuba's dad drove his builder's van into the car park. Reject Rovers stared out of the windows in horror.

'Strike me!' said Mr Turnbull. 'Look at these crowds. There must be a big game on today.'

'There is, Dad,' said Scuba miserably. 'They've all come to see us lose.'

'Oh no! There's Amanda Ross from our class,' said Kevin, ducking down behind a seat. Grinning faces pressed up against the van windows.

'Gonna lose! Gonna lose! Gonna lose!' they chanted.

Rovers pushed their way through the jeering crowds to the changing rooms.

They were just unpacking their kit when there was a knock on the door. Sean Slack came in.

'What do you want, Slack? Your changing room's next door,' said Kevin.

'That's not very sporting, Taylor. I just came to wish you good luck,' Slack protested.

'You just did. Now goodbye,' said Kevin.

But Slack insisted on going round to each of the team one by one. He shook their hands and hoped they played well.

What was going on? As Kevin laced up his boots, he wondered what his enemy was up to.

'Hey, what are you doing with my gloves?'
It was Scuba who cried out.

Slack turned round. 'Nothing! Just having a look,' he said, innocently.

He handed the red goalkeeper's gloves back to Scuba. 'Nice gloves,' he said. 'I bet you're just *itching* to get in goal. Ha ha!'

Scuba looked at him as if he'd got a screw loose. Slack paused at the door. 'Well, good luck again, lads. You'll need it. Especially you, Taylor. My boots are going to get so, so muddy today.'

He put out his tongue and licked his lips.

Kevin turned his face to the wall. He felt he was going to be sick. Scuba and Alex were the only ones he'd told about the bet. But all the others had heard it from Slack anyway.

Five minutes later there was a second knock on the door. This time they all shouted, 'Get lost, Slack!'

'It's only me,' said Alex's voice. 'Are you all changed? I thought we'd have a team talk.'

Looking round the changing room, Alex could see how nervous they all were. Rovers were used to playing in front of two or three people (one of them always reading the newspaper). But today there was a big crowd waiting for them. Everyone from school had come to see them lose.

Kevin was already panicking and Scuba couldn't stop scratching himself.

Alex did her best to calm their nerves.

'Forget the crowd,' she said. 'Forget how good the other side are. All you have to think about is yourselves. Today is your chance to shock them all. Show them Rovers are a football team, not a big joke. I know you can do it. I've seen you in training. Let's hear you say it again.

'"We're Rovers. We're winners. We're the best."'

They chanted it. Loud. Three times. Then they ran out onto the pitch.

A great cheer went up. Looking round, Kevin saw there were crowds on every side of the pitch. Even his mum and sister – who hated football – had come. He saw Steve Ryan from *The Grimley Gazette*. There was the TV crew behind their goal.

Kevin tried to calm his nerves by taking practice shots at Scuba.

But Scuba was in an even worse state. He kept removing his gloves to scratch at his hands.

'What's up?' asked Kevin.

'I don't know. It's my hands. They feel like they're on fire.'

At the other end of the pitch, Sean Slack and Miles Elliot were watching.

'It's working,' laughed Miles. 'Look, he's scratching himself like a dog.'

'I'm not surprised,' said Slack. 'I gave him the whole tin. Half in each glove.' Slack paused to thump a ball into the corner of the net. 'The game's in the bag,' he said.

A minute later they were lining up for the kick-off.

This is it, thought Kevin with the ball at his feet. The crowd were hushed.

'Come on the Dynamos!' called someone.

'Come on the clodhoppers!' shouted someone else.

There were roars of laughter.

The referee blew his whistle.

Kevin passed to Persil. Persil knocked it back to Stringbean. Stringbean passed to Baby Joe out on the wing.

He beat two players, got to the line and crossed, the way Alex had showed him. Dynamos' keeper leapt and caught it, but the crowd had stopped laughing. They weren't expecting Rovers to go on the attack. They had come to see them buried under an avalanche of goals.

For the first twenty minutes Rovers held their own. They got ten players back to defend. They tackled hard. They passed the ball so that Dynamos had to work to get it back. They were playing well – apart from their goalkeeper who was behaving very oddly.

Scuba couldn't keep still. One minute his gloves were on, then they were off again. He danced around his goal as if ants were invading his shorts. Then disaster struck.

Sean Slack got the ball just outside the penalty area. He looked up and saw Scuba bending down to pick up his gloves. Slack let fly a stinging shot. It whistled over Scuba's head and into the top corner of the goal.

The crowd cheered and laughed. This was what they'd come to see – the Rejects playing like clowns.

'What are you doing?' hissed Kevin as he took the ball from Scuba.

'I can't help it,' Scuba groaned, miserably. 'My hands are itching like mad. I think it's these gloves.'

Kevin carried the ball back to kick-off.

'That's it,' Persil told him gloomily, 'we'll never get back in the game now. We're going to get slaughtered.'

The soft goal had knocked the confidence out of Rovers. They soon lost the ball. Eastley Dynamos won a corner. It came over in the air and Scuba jumped to meet it. The ball floated straight into his waiting gloves. Then he fumbled it. Sean Slack was on hand to boot it gleefully into the roof of the net.

2-0 to Dynamos.

Scuba wished he could dig himself a deep hole. He imagined the goal being replayed in slow motion on the local TV news that night.

Rovers had let in two goals in two minutes. They were starting to look like their old selves.

For the rest of the half they booted the ball anywhere to clear it. Dynamos hit the post and then the crossbar.

Rovers rode their luck and were relieved to hear the half-time whistle.

Alex called them together in the centre circle.

'What happened? You were playing so well. Then you went to pieces!'

'It's Scuba,' said Kevin. 'We'd still be in the game if it wasn't for him. Now they're all over us.' The others nodded in agreement.

Scuba stood there in misery, scratching at his wrists. 'I can't help it!' he moaned. 'Look at my hands, they've gone all red! Someone's put something in my gloves.' He showed them the orange dust caked inside.

Kevin had seen something like it in a joke shop. 'It's itching powder!' he said. 'It must have been Sean Slack, the dirty cheat! He was messing with Scuba's gloves when he came into our changing room. Wait till I get him!'

Alex had to hold Kevin back.

'It's no good starting a fight,' she said. 'You'll just get yourself sent off. The only way to deal with cheats is to beat them at their own game. Go out there and get back in the match. Scuba, you can't play in goal with hands like that. You swap with Stringbean.'

'What, me? Play in goal?' Stringbean stared at Alex.

'You told me you were good at basketball.'

'Yes, but that's different.'

'You'll be fine. Just use those long arms of yours. Now the game's not over yet. You're only two goals down. Let's show Sean Slack he isn't going to get away with this.'

Kevin nodded. He glanced at Scuba who was busy turning his gloves inside out.

'What are you doing now?'

'I've got an idea. Alex is right. You've got to play cheats at their own game.'

'What are you on about, Scuba?'

'There's still plenty of powder in these gloves.' He put them on, inside out. 'I'll be back in a minute,' he said, and trotted over towards Eastley Dynamos.

Kevin shook his head. Scuba had finally flipped. He watched him go up to Sean Slack and slap him hard on the back of the neck.

'Well played, Sean. Great goal!' said Scuba.

Slack glared at him, scornfully. 'I've only just started. We're going to murder you this half!'

Scuba gave him a cheery wave. Then he went round the rest of the Dynamos team, slapping and rubbing them on the back to congratulate them.

'What was all that about?' asked Kevin, when Scuba trotted back.

'You'll see. Just giving them a hand!' Scuba took up his position in defence.

The game restarted. Dynamos went on the attack looking for more easy goals.

Slack took a pass with his back to goal. Skilfully, he turned past Scuba and pushed the ball between Dangerous's legs. Slack now had the goal at his mercy. There was only Stringbean to beat. But, just as he was about to shoot, he clawed at the back of his neck.

'Yahhh! Oww! It stings!' Slack hopped around as if bitten by a viper. Meanwhile, Scuba calmly took the ball away from him.

'Tut tut! Nasty stuff, itching powder,' he said, shaking his head.

Rovers took the ball upfield. Dynamos tried to get it back, but now odd things were happening all over the pitch. Eastley players were pulling off their shirts and scratching furiously at their backs.

The ball came to Kevin – he slipped it inside to Baby Joe. The Dynamos keeper came out, then had to pause to itch his neck. Baby Joe dribbled round him and scored; 2-1.

The crowd cheered and Rovers celebrated their first goal in fifteen games.

Scuba gave Kevin a thumbs-up with the gloves. 'Told you I'd give them a hand.'

'Come on Rovers, get a second!' shouted Alex, jumping up and down with excitement.

Eastley Dynamos had gone to pieces. The itching powder Scuba had spread around was affecting half their team. And the other half were keeping well away from Scuba.

Kevin went down the wing and passed inside to Scuba. Scuba advanced to the edge of the penalty area. Three Eastley defenders blocked his path to goal – but none of them wanted to risk a tackle. They seemed to be hypnotized by Scuba's deadly powdered gloves. While they hesitated, Scuba pushed the ball past them and tried a shot.

It scudded along the ground, hit a bump in front of the diving keeper, and bounced over him into the goal. Miraculously, Rovers were level.

As Dynamos kicked off, Kevin could see the wonder on his team-mates' faces. They thought they'd done it, that the game was over. But Kevin knew that for him, it wasn't enough. They had to win or he would still lose his bet with Slack.

The thought of licking dirt from Slack's boots in front of everyone was too much to bear. He'd rather lie down in a bathful of maggots.

There were only fifteen minutes left. Rovers needed one more goal but their old failings started to show. Kevin shot over the bar from five yards out and Persil fluffed an easy chance by waiting too long.

The effect of the itching powder was starting to wear off. Sean Slack looked dangerous at the other end. He would have scored twice if Stringbean's long arms and legs hadn't got in the way.

It was a nail-biting finish with the crowd urging both sides forward to get the winner.

Kevin chased the ball all over the pitch in desperation. As the final minutes ticked away, Rovers won a corner.

Just as they'd practised in training, Persil crossed and Kevin jumped to head it. He was going to score. Until someone shoved him in the back and he went sprawling.

'Tough luck, Taylor!' grinned Slack, standing over him. Slack's grin melted away when the referee's whistle blew. He'd seen the push and awarded Rovers a penalty.

There was one problem. No one wanted to take it. The Rovers players remembered too well their pictures in *The Grimley Gazette*. When Kevin offered them the ball they all shook their heads.

'Why don't you take it?' suggested Scuba.

'Me? Why me?' asked Kevin.

'You're the captain. It's your job.'

'But I'll panic. I'm bound to miss, I know I will.'

The referee blew his whistle again, impatiently.

'Go on. You can do it, Kevin,' said Scuba.

Kevin placed the ball on the spot. So it all came down to this. One shot. Just him and the goalkeeper. If he missed they would all blame him – Kevin 'Panic' Taylor – but not as much as he would blame himself.

He glanced up at the faces crowding behind the goal for a better view. There were his mum and sister, his classmates from school, and the TV camera zooming in on him. All waiting for him to miss.

90

He felt the panic rising from somewhere in his stomach. He couldn't look at the goal. It would be shrinking smaller and smaller.

He tried to concentrate on the ball. If he could just kick it in the right direction so that he didn't look totally stupid …

Just as he was about to start his run-up, a sneering voice said, 'Whoops! Missed again, Kevin!'

Without looking, Kevin knew the voice was Slack's. He felt a rush of fury.

He ran at the ball and thumped it with all his might. It went high and to his left.

Dynamos' goalkeeper flung himself and got one hand to it. For an awful moment, Kevin thought the goalkeeper had saved it. But the power of the shot took it past his fingertips and into the net.

There was a moment of stunned silence all round the pitch. Then the noise erupted.

Kevin was buried under a pile of players jumping on top of him. Alex was hugging everyone in the crowd, people she'd never met. Sean Slack was chasing his own goalkeeper round the pitch.

When the game finally re-started, it only lasted a minute longer. The referee blew his whistle. Rovers had won. It was unbelievable.

They had beaten Eastley Dynamos. They wouldn't be claiming a place in the record books. They weren't The Worst Team in History. As Alex said afterwards, 'Even Man United would have been proud of that performance.'

Kevin was mobbed by friends from school. They all said that they knew Rovers could do it all along.

The TV people wanted an interview with him.

'Kevin, that was a shock result,' said the reporter. 'How do you explain the difference in your team today?'

'Teamwork,' said Kevin. 'Thanks to our new manager, Alex, we've been improving all the time. The best is yet to come,' he added with a grin.

'Did you always believe you could do it?'

'Of course,' said Kevin. 'In fact I had a bet on the result with someone. About a pair of boots.'

Kevin took off one of his football boots and held it up. It was caked in oozing brown mud.

'Has anyone seen Sean Slack? I've got something for him.'

Hiding in the middle of the crowd, Sean Slack gulped. He tried to wriggle his way out, keeping his head down. But Scuba was watching and grabbed him by the arm.

'Come on, Slack,' he said. 'The cameras are waiting. Now it's your turn to make history.'

About the author

The idea for this story started with an article I came across in a newspaper. It was about an utterly hopeless men's football team who had lost a record number of games in a row. It started me thinking what it  would be like to play for the worst team in the world. Reject Rovers are a bit like some of the teams I played for when I was at school – so bad they can only get better!